Old DUMFRIES

by
David Carroll

Buchan's Preserves and Confectionery Works on the Annan Road. These premises were originally occupied by the Drummond car firm, builders of custom-made cars, and the jam factory moved to the site between the wars. Following the Second World War, however, the building served as council stores before being taken over by a local building firm. Nowadays the site is occupied by a complex which provides residential and day-care facilities under the aegis of Community Integrated Care.

BURNS GRAND DAUGHTER (MRS BROWN) AND GREAT GRAND
DAUGHTER (MISS JEAN ARMOUR BURNS BROWN) AT THE
HOUSE WHEREIN THE POET DIED, DUMFRIES.
"THE BURNS STUDIO SERIES, AYR." "COPYRIGHT."

© David Carroll 2000
First published in the United Kingdom, 2000,
by Stenlake Publishing Ltd.
Telephone: 01290 551122

ISBN 1 84033 129 1

FURTHER READING

The books listed below were used by the author during his research. They are
not available from Stenlake Publishing. Those interested in finding out more are
advised to contact their local bookshop or reference library.

Desmond Donaldson, *Bygone Dumfries and Galloway*, 4 vols., M. Anderson,
1976–1979.
William McDowall, *History of Dumfries*, EP Publishing, 1972 (reprinted from
1906 edition).

ACKNOWLEDGEMENTS

I am particularly indebted to Bernadette Walsh, without whose help this book
would almost certainly not have been completed.
The publishers would like to thank Ian MacDowall for providing additional
pictures for the book.

This postcard showing Robert Burns's granddaughter, and his great-
granddaughter Miss Jean Armour Burns Brown (left) is dated 1905, and bears the
following message from its sender: 'I have just spoken to this old lady and her
daughter and obtained quite a lot of information a la Burns'. The two ladies are
standing at the entrance to Burns House in Burns Street (see page 20), thus
bestowing on the place a pleasing sense of continuity with their illustrious forbear.
Jean Armour Burns Brown was Burns's last surviving descendant to live in
Dumfries, and died in 1937. She bore a striking resemblance to the poet, and
capitalised on their similar appearance by having herself painted in exactly the
same style as the famous Alexander Nasmyth portrait of Burns. She even imitated
her ancestor's hairstyle and clothing, so that to the layman the two pictures are
hard to tell apart at first glance.

INTRODUCTION

As if anticipating a survey published only a few years ago which revealed that Dumfries was the second most desirable place to live in Britain (Sheffield, I believe, came top of the list), the irascible Squire Bramble in Tobias Smollett's novel *The Expedition of Humphry Clinker* (1771) declared that if he had to make his home anywhere in Scotland then it would certainly be in Dumfries. He described it as 'A very elegant trading town near the borders of England,' adding that 'the accommodation [is] as good in all respects as in any part of South Britain.'

With over 30,000 inhabitants, Dumfries is the largest community in the thinly-populated south-west of Scotland, but is thought to have begun life as little more than a cluster of huts set close to what is now the area around Nith Place. In its time the town has been the scene of pioneering attempts in the use of anaesthetics for surgical operations and, on a more sombre note, Scotland's last public execution was carried out at the old prison in Buccleuch Street during the 1860s. When, in the early years of the twentieth century, Arrol-Johnston began manufacturing its luxury motor cars on the outskirts of Dumfries, the town was quickly dubbed 'a little Detroit by the Nith'. Much of the town's nineteenth century prosperity, however, was based on the tweed mills, which employed around 1,400 local people at the industry's height. After the decline of the mills, substantial firms such as Nestlé, ICI and what later became the Gates Rubber Company moved into the town.

Once a considerable port, with a succession of quays stretching down to the Solway Firth, Dumfries is bisected by the Nith, and from either side of the river many of the town's narrow streets rise and fall in steep and disconcertingly straight lines. For centuries the river served as an effective natural boundary separating Dumfries from neighbouring Maxwelltown. A 1930s local guidebook explains that 'in olden times, Maxwelltown was known as the Brig-en' of Dumfries. It was notorious for the lawlessness of its inhabitants, and had the reputation of being one of the worst places in the kingdom. It was so bad that a well-known London magistrate said he could trace a rogue over the whole kingdom, but always lost him at the Brig-en' of Dumfries or in the Gorbals of Glasgow. Things are very much different nowadays,' the guidebook concludes, 'and the old Brig-en' claims to be the West End of Dumfries.' The two burghs were amalgamated in 1929, and many 'doonhamers' would still aver that this was one of the most controversial events in the history of the town that was created a Royal Burgh in 1186. A strong sense of independent identity, rooted in an age-old allegiance to one side of the river or the other, persists to this day.

Four bridges span the Nith along Whitesands, a broad and busy artery beside the river, and once the scene every autumn of the boisterous Rood Fair and noisy auctions. The New Bridge, opened in 1794 and so-called to distinguish it from Devorgilla's Bridge a few yards downstream, links Buccleuch Street with Galloway Street. But it is the older bridge (rebuilt from an earlier timber affair) which is much more pleasing to the eye. Constructed, like much of Dumfries, from red sandstone, it is the oldest surviving multiple-arched stone bridge in Scotland and owes its existence to the generosity of Lady Devorgilla, a daughter of the first Lord of Galloway who was married to the founder of Balliol College, Oxford. Floodlit at dusk, the six arches of Devorgilla's Bridge, drenched in amber light, are one of the town's most pleasing features. An imposing nineteenth-century suspension bridge and the comparatively modern St Michael's Bridge, opened in the 1920s, complete the quartet.

It is impossible to stray far in Dumfries without being reminded that Robert Burns is intricately woven into the fabric of the place. To begin with, a statue of the great man, worked in Carrara marble by Amelia Hill, occupies a commanding position at the busy junction of High Street, Buccleuch Street and Church Crescent. In addition, some of the town's oldest and most distinctive buildings have close associations with him.

Take the Midsteeple, for example, which presides over the High Street. Completed in 1707 and restored in 1909, it has served over the years as a municipal building, courthouse and prison. In June each year it is the scene of a major highlight in the Guid Nychburris festival – a week-long celebration that has its origins in medieval days, but which in its present form dates only from the 1930s – when the 'Queen of the South' is crowned in the shadow of the ancient building. The ceremony always draws a large crowd on a day when the whole town is *en fête*.

The Midsteeple was also an important gathering point during the eighteenth century for the cattle drovers of Galloway, who paused there while taking their beasts on the long and arduous journey south to market. As a reminder of those days, a table of distances placed on one wall lists, among other diverse destinations, Portpatrick and Huntingdon; the latter being the location from which much Scottish beef found its way to London.

On a July night in 1796, the body of Robert Burns lay virtually 'in state' at the Midsteeple, as a prelude to his funeral the following day. The route to St Michael's churchyard, where the poet was buried, took the impressive cortège within a stone's throw of the Globe Inn, the bard's favourite 'howff', as he famously called it. The Globe has been a hostelry since 1610 and, tucked away in its tight little close off the High Street, the whitewashed stone building retains much of its original atmosphere. The old stables have now been incorporated into the inn but, apart from that, a number of the rooms are just as they were in the poet's day.

In a land where the term 'bard' is synonymous with Burns, it is nevertheless fitting that Scotland's oldest working theatre should occupy a spot in Shakespeare Street. The Theatre Royal has endured a chequered history. Now the home of the town's amateur company, the Guild of Players, the Theatre Royal began life in 1792. Burns was one of its earliest patrons, and in the 1840s the great tragedian William Charles Macready (whose father had leased the theatre some years earlier), played Hamlet and Shylock there on successive nights. Three decades later a youthful J. M. Barrie, then a pupil at Dumfries Academy, was a regular member of the audience, and in later life fondly recalled that the theatre was 'so tiny that you smile to it as to a child when you go in.' The Theatre Royal's star waned at the beginning of the twentieth century, and the building was used as an auction room for some years before enjoying a brief spell as a cinema. By the mid-1950s it was closed and scheduled for demolition, but the Guild of Players acquired the property in 1959 and raised the necessary funds to restore it. Recently the building has undergone another thorough refurbishment and it has rarely looked more attractive.

Whereas some towns are noted, perhaps, for their antique shops or bookshops, Dumfries is particularly well-endowed with a range of local museums which reflect the diverse nature of the community and its windswept surroundings. Visitors will not be surprised to find that the house where Burns spent the last few years of his life is now open to the public. Burns House, with its rich red sandstone façade, is an essential port of call for anyone with the remotest interest in the life and work of the poet.

More unusual is the Crichton Museum, situated in the extensive and supremely well-manicured grounds of the Crichton Royal Hospital. The museum charts the history and progress of an institution that – founded in 1839 – soon achieved an enviable worldwide reputation for its enlightened treatment of people with mental health problems. The Aviation Museum, housed in a former control tower on the town's disused airfield, together with a museum of town life occupying the tiny Bridge House (possibly the oldest domestic building in Dumfries) on the Maxwelltown side of the river, are also unlooked-for gems.

The overall prize, however, must be awarded to Dumfries Museum itself. Sited in the tower of an eighteenth-century stone windmill at the top of Corberry Hill, and founded in 1835 as a combined astronomical observatory and museum, it is certainly the most distinctive feature on the town's western skyline. The complex has been extended over the years to accommodate a collection that now represents the whole of Dumfries and Galloway.

Understandably, the museum's greatest attraction is the camera obscura, the oldest obscura of its type still in use in the world. It has captured more than a century and a half of the town's everyday life by the simple expedient of projecting moving images on to a blank screen in a dark room; images that have ranged from shipping on the Nith during the 1830s to traffic congestion along Whitesands in this new millennium. The camera obscura offers everyone an opportunity to explore the town that has been affectionately christened 'Queen of the South'.

Looking up Bank Street towards High Street from the Whitesands end, *c.*1920. During Burns's time, when the poet lived with his family on one floor of the tenement shown near left, this thoroughfare was officially called the Wee Vennel, although in that age of open sewers it was known locally as the Stinking Vennel! The Bank Street flat (the building in question is still standing but is privately owned and **not** open to the public) must have seemed very cramped to Burns and his family after their more spacious rural quarters at Ellisland Farm. However, Burns still managed to complete over 60 poems and songs during his eighteen months' residence there (from November 1791 to May 1793) and a plaque on the wall, put up in 1971, proclaims it the 'Songhouse of Scotland'.

Annan Road looking west *c*.1912, with St Mary's church in the far distance. Prior to the opening of the town's bypass in the early 1990s, Annan Road was the main route into Dumfries for travellers approaching from the east.

Academy Street *c.*1912. The iron railings mark the perimeter of the academy itself, an institution that was much extended along the left-hand side of the road during the years leading up to the Second World War (when it was destined to serve as the county's central secondary school), and which in earlier days had numbered among its more famous pupils the playwright J. M. Barrie. The author of *Peter Pan* studied in the old academy building, however, which was demolished in 1897 and replaced by what a contemporary local guidebook described as a 'handsome building of classical design'; a structure which still forms part of the academy complex today.

Looking along English Street which, in the 1930s, was described by a local guidebook as 'one of the narrowest and also one of the busiest thoroughfares in the town.' No change there then, except that today the traffic all flies in the same direction along what forms part of the town's one-way system. Jubilee Buildings, with its drab bust of Queen Victoria set into the wall, stands on the near left corner. This was once the home of the curiously-named County Toilet Club, with its 'haircutting, shaving and shampooing saloons'; all a far cry from the retailers of hi-tech equipment who have occupied the premises over recent years.

The village of Gasstown grew up in the early nineteenth century to the east of Dumfries, and was named after Joseph Gass (a former provost of the town) who did much to encourage and assist its development. The houses seen here on the Annan Road constituted the Front Row, with Mid Row cutting in between and Back Row running along behind. These names and a few of Gasstown's old cottages still survive among the large modern schemes of houses and bungalows that sprang up as the town expanded in this area. The corner house of what was called the 'top half' of Front Row (near left) was occupied by Dobson's general store and post office when this photograph was taken in the early 1900s.

THE NEW BRIDGE. DUMFRIES.

The New (or Buccleuch) Bridge, pictured here a few years before it was strengthened and improved in 1935. These cattle were probably on their way to be sold at one of the indoor marts on Whitesands. Completed in 1794 and designed by local architect Thomas Boyd, the bridge linked what were then the neighbouring burghs of Dumfries and Maxwelltown (the two burghs were amalgamated in 1929). Its construction led to a significant expansion of the town in this area. As the years wore on, this bridge became the main route for heavy goods vehicles making their way through Dumfries to the ferry terminal at Stranraer. However, the weight of traffic crossing the river at this point – and the resulting congestion, particularly along Whitesands – has eased considerably since the opening of the town's bypass in the early 1990s.

Buccleuch Street, laid out in the early 1790s and opened to traffic in 1795, is one of the town's most elegant and well-proportioned thoroughfares. At the time it was constructed, Buccleuch Street provided a marked contrast with the crowded courts and closes that existed in other parts of the town. This view, taken from the bridge and looking up towards Greyfriars' church in the early 1900s, is easily recognisable today. Leading off and running behind Buccleuch Street on the left, the lesser byways of Charlotte Street, George Street and Castle Street all contributed to the new-found Regency style of this more sedate quarter.

The most distinctive architectural feature to catch the eye in Buccleuch Street is the Sheriff Court House with its lofty pointed towers, a building erected – as William McDowall's *History of Dumfries* tells us – in the Scottish Baronial style, and opened in time for the spring assizes of April 1866. 'Whenever the turrets of the edifice are seen mingling in the sky outline of the burgh,' McDowall eulogises, 'they look exceedingly striking and picturesque . . . The entire building has a superb appearance whether viewed from the street or surveyed from a distant height.' The old county prison stood on the near left (the site latterly occupied by the Clydesdale Bank) and it was here – in 1868 – that Scotland's last public execution was carried out, with the gallows on display for all to see. The hanging of Robert Smith, a rapist and murderer, drew a crowd of over 600 people from the town and outlying districts.

This view of the High Street, probably dating from the 1920s, is dominated by one of the town's great historic landmarks, the Midsteeple, with Greyfriars' church in the background. The Coffee House Hotel, glimpsed on the right, was later demolished and a new building erected on the site for the tailoring chain of Montague Burton. Completed in 1707 and restored in 1909, the Midsteeple has been a municipal building, courthouse and prison over the years. Its precincts have always been a natural gathering point for the townspeople on special occasions; a place of festival and ceremony. The Queensberry Monument can be seen to the right of the Midsteeple. Designed by Robert Adam and erected in 1778, it was removed in 1935 and placed in front of the County Buildings in English Street. In 1990, however, the column was restored to its original site.

Horse and trap appears to have been the favoured method of locomotion around 1914, when this photograph of the High Street looking towards Greyfriars and the Burns statue was taken. Most of the individual shops and businesses pictured here (such as Brash, the grocers), which gave the town its own unique flavour, have disappeared and – as elsewhere around the country – the high street multiples have moved in to replace them. However, the Hole I' the Wa' Inn is a notable exception and remains a thriving watering-hole today. Established in 1620, it was doubtless one of the hostelries frequented by Burns when he lived in the town, although not so closely associated with him as the Globe, for example. However, that fact did not deter John Thomson, a late-nineteenth century proprietor of the inn, from amassing an impressive collection of Burnsiana which was displayed in the public bar at one time, and which included the poet's Dumfries Burgess ticket, his excise swordstick and – more prosaically perhaps – his teapot and caddy.

The south end of the High Street (now pedestrianised), is dominated by the ornate fountain dating from 1882 which stands at the junction with English Street. On hot summer days the fine spray which cascades around it acts as a magnet for anyone seeking the lightest but coolest of showers. The present fountain replaced an earlier one built on the site to commemorate the introduction of water to Dumfries in 1851. This was piped in from Lochrutton Loch four miles west of the town. On the left the elegant King's Arms Hotel, once Dumfries's principal coaching inn, presides over the scene, although as with the County Hotel (formerly the Commercial) opposite, it is no longer in existence. MacGowan & Co., drapers, silk mercers, clothiers, hatters and shirtmakers (near right) was, according to an old trade directory, 'one of the fashionable centres of the town, favourable with anything of the kind in the kingdom.'

Friars' Vennel in the early 1900s. It is hard to believe that before the development of nearby Buccleuch Street and the construction of the New Bridge this narrow, slightly shabby and decidedly claustrophobic aperture running down from Church Place and the High Street to Whitesands was one of the town's principal thoroughfares. Despite many proposals and attempts to rectify the situation, properties at the foot of the Vennel are still liable to flooding when the Nith seriously bursts its banks, and it is not unknown for rowing boats to have been pressed into service on the most extreme occasions.

Looking down Friars' Vennel towards the Nith in the 1930s, with Maxwelltown beyond.

The view up Friars' Vennel towards the High Street and Church Place. Until the end of the eighteenth century the Vennel extended across the High Street to St Andrew's Street. Greyfriars' monastery, which gave this thoroughfare its name, covered an area extending from the top left-hand side of this photograph, and included a church, dormitory, granary and refectory. 'The most momentous historical event in the annals of Dumfries,' proclaimed a 1930s' guidebook, 'was the murder of Comyn by Bruce in Greyfriars' monastery, [when] the two Scottish leaders quarrelled, and Bruce drew his dagger and stabbed Comyn beside the high altar.'

Looking along Church Street, Maxwelltown, from the Market Square end in the early 1900s. The road rises steeply from here towards the Observatory but, although a vestige of the bend remains, the area has changed out of all recognition since this photograph was taken. Blocks of flats have replaced the houses pictured here, and the effect has been to broaden out this once narrow and cramped thoroughfare. The viewpoint is probably from the end of Howgate Street with the entrance to Maxwell Street – again much altered – on the right.

Terregles Street c.1912, looking towards Galloway Street and Laurieknowe. The building on the near left, erected in 1893, was originally Maxwelltown's combined courthouse and police station complete with cells. Note the bobby's bicycle leaning against the wall. The far end of the building served as the station sergeant's living accommodation, while a separate block at the rear was used as married quarters for the constables. The water board occupied these premises for a while after the Second World War, but in recent years they have been converted into private flats. Present-day Terregles Street is more or less recognisable in the view seen here. The cobbles have disappeared, of course, together with the low buildings on the far left, but much remains intact. Dumfries Prison, just a stone's throw from Terregles Street, opened in 1883 and the imposing sandstone house whose front garden (with ornate lamp crowning the gateway) can just be glimpsed on the near right, served as living quarters for the warders.

Burns House. The poet lived at this house in what is now called Burns Street (formerly Mill Street) from May 1793 until his death in July 1796. Built of local red sandstone, the façade of the house was later plastered over as is clearly shown here. In 1934, however, as part of an extensive restoration programme to the property, the plaster was painstakingly chipped away by council workmen, thus allowing the original stonework to be seen once again. The house, which serves as a museum devoted to Burns's life and work, inevitably attracts visitors and literary pilgrims from around the world. Original letters and manuscripts are housed here, together with the famous Kilmarnock and Edinburgh editions of Burns's work. There are some touching items of memorabilia too, such as the chair in which he is said to have composed his last poems, and the gun he carried when out on excise duties.

Away from the horrors of the trenches, these convalescent soldiers are enjoying a leisurely trip in a rowing boat on the Nith *c*.1916. The separate burghs of Dumfries and Maxwelltown had three Red Cross hospitals during the First World War, catering for the needs of servicemen who required treatment and recuperation. The Dumfries hospital was situated in Lovers' Walk, while those in Maxwelltown were in Laurieknowe (the building was originally the Maxwelltown Free Church) and Broomlands (now demolished) on the New Abbey Road.

Convalescent Soldiers boating on the Nith, Dumfries. 81

The café at the Crichton Royal Hospital's Easterbrook Hall, photographed when the building – an impressive complex embracing a large recreation hall, library, occupational therapy department, operating theatre, gymnasium and many other facilities – opened in 1938. The café offered refreshments to patients, staff and visitors. Patients who were unable to handle conventional money were provided with tokens. Universally known as 'the canteen', it served as a tea-room and shop until 1990, when Easterbrook Hall was taken over to accommodate the lengthy enquiry into the Lockerbie bombing. The café reopened at nearby Johnston House before moving to its present home in Crichton Hall.

The caul, which extends across the Nith from near the foot of Friars' Vennel, was constructed to provide more water power for the town's old grain mill (later rebuilt and now housing the Robert Burns Centre), by raising the water-level immediately upstream behind it. In 1911 the mill was converted into a hydroelectric station, and the force of water gushing down the caul could be harnessed to provide sufficient electricity to power the town's street lighting. When the water-level dropped dramatically, however, the lights grew dimmer. William McDowall mentions that fishery proprietors in the higher reaches of the Nith opposed the construction of the caul, 'contending that it would prevent salmon from running up the river as formerly.' Originally there had been a ford across the river roughly where the caul is situated. It was much used by pilgrims who passed through the town en route for Whithorn.

Market day on Whitesands *c.*1912. An early-nineteenth century account of the town states that 'Dumfries has long been celebrated for its markets, which are held every Wednesday, when a great deal of business is done among the cattle dealers upon the Sands.' Writing just over a hundred years later, by which time most of this business had been transferred to indoor marts nearby, another commentator observed that Whitesands had for long been 'the site of the greatest weekly market for cattle in Scotland. Enormous herds of black Galloways were disposed of in the autumn and sent to the rich pastures of the south.' However, the growth of the railways put paid to the old droving methods which had made Dumfries such a focal point for the region's cattle dealers, and by the time this photograph was taken the much altered and reduced open-air market on Whitesands dealt mainly with pigs and horses.

Horse Fair, Dumfries.

A horse fair on Whitesands in the early 1900s. Horse fairs were usually held on the Sands twice a year – in February and October – and attracted a large number of dealers and animals. 'The number of all kinds [of horses] exposed may perhaps vary from 400 to 600,' estimated a mid-nineteenth century survey. 'A portion of the best draught horses are retained for service in the district in which they have been reared,' it continued, 'and the surplus carried by dealers to Edinburgh and Glasgow, the West Country generally and to the north of England.' With the introduction of tractors and motorised transport, however, the use of horses in agriculture and other areas of work rapidly declined, and fairs of the kind pictured here soon became a thing of the past.

The Rood Fair in the early 1900s. J. Hutcheon, writing in *The County of Dumfries*, gives an interesting account of the event as it appeared in the 1950s. 'Held about the last week in September,' he explains, 'the town council clings to its ancient right of letting the Whitesands to the showmen and, for a week, about one third of a mile of the Sands between the Old Bridge and the Dock Park are devoted to shows. The character of the fair is greatly changed. It now largely consists of sideshows with a few merry-go-rounds and their modern counterparts, a boxing booth and a circus.' This scene shows just how eagerly-anticipated an event the Rood Fair was, not only by Dumfries folk but by those who flocked into the town from the outlying villages to savour the festive atmosphere. It was an important holiday occasion and people dressed up for it accordingly.

Whitesands has always been the main departure point for those buses serving the surrounding towns and villages, as well as for further-afield services. This photograph shows the vehicles reversed against the pavement, a practise that only ceased within the last five years or so with the construction of properly laid-out bus stances (nearly 50 years after the idea had first been suggested). Unlike today, when many of the region's routes are in the hands of one large company (although a number of private family firms remain), the buses and motor-coaches lined up here would have been owned largely by individual operators – some of them fighting for passengers on the same routes – and competition for trade was fierce. For example, the buses in the right foreground were owned by Clark of Southerness for their route from there to Dumfries, while the bus approaching belonged to Sword's Midland Bus Service of Airdrie operating the long service to Glasgow. An earlier incarnation of the present-day Whitesands car park can be glimpsed in the background.

The Troqueer and Rosefield Mills on the Maxwelltown side of the Nith, c.1911. 'Too often elsewhere,' wrote William McDowall, 'town factories are dull, dingy, repulsive-looking erections; but in pleasing contrast to all this . . . the Troqueer establishment is in every way a great acquisition to the suburbs of Maxwelltown.' He went on to add that the Rosefield Mill 'presents a compact, harmonious whole.' By 1872, when the town's mills were arguably the largest producers of tweed in Scotland, 1,400 people were employed in the industry locally. 'To estimate the beneficial results that flow to the town from the tweed trade would be no easy task,' McDowall went on. 'But for these, and the stimulus given to other occupations by the railways, Dumfries, instead of advancing steadily and rapidly . . . would undoubtedly have retrograded, both as regards population and wealth.' However, trade declined rapidly following the First World War and the Troqueer Mill closed after a fire in 1923. Rosefield Mill staggered on through the Depression years but closed just before the outbreak of the Second World War.

Mill workers returning to Dumfries from Maxwelltown, using the impressive suspension bridge that was erected over the Nith for their benefit (and which opened in 1875), thus saving them the inconvenience of having to walk further upstream to cross by the Old Bridge. When people walked over the suspension bridge in large groups such as this, the whole contraption shook (just like the Millennium Bridge in London!). Occasionally, fears were raised about its safety and in February 1911, following another wave of concern, the *Dumfries and Galloway Standard* reported that 'during the past few days work has been carried out [on the bridge], the purpose of which was to secure greater rigidity . . . There has since been, as was to be expected, more vibration but there is no cause for apprehension.' If you tread hard enough when crossing the bridge today you can still feel a slight movement. The bridge is a particularly attractive sight at Christmas, when it is lit with coloured bulbs along the whole of its length.

A vessel discharging its cargo at Dock Foot. The *Statistical Account* for 1833 records that imports were principally coal, slate, iron, tallow, timber, hemp and wine, while exports included wool, freestone, oats, wheat and barley, with vessels plying regularly between Liverpool, Maryport and Whitehaven. However, shipping trade steadily declined from the mid-nineteenth century, partly owing to the coming of the railway but also because larger vessels began to experience difficulties when navigating the river beyond Glencaple. A century later, a further *Statistical Account* explained that it was 'its melancholy duty to report that Dumfries has entirely lost her proud title of a seaport. Until a few years ago . . . two or three ships a year unloaded supplies for local merchants; this has now ceased.' The port of Dumfries extended down the Nith to include Kingholm Quay, Glencaple and Carsethorn. The last vessel to berth at Dock Foot did so in 1916.

The royal parks in London are said to be the lungs of the capital, and Dock Park performs the same function for the town of Dumfries. In March 1795 the Royal Dumfries Volunteers, raised (with Burns as a founder-member, incidentally) to defend the town against any possible incursions by Bonaparte and his army, met here for their inaugural parade and drill. In recent times, however, Dock Park has served a more recreational purpose. A 1930s' guidebook describes it as a place 'where the weary traveller will have no difficulty in finding a seat on which to rest and, at the same time, admire the beauty of the surroundings.' As this late 1920s' photograph demonstrates, the more energetic were able to play tennis on one of Dock Park's four public courts.

Bowling has been a popular activity in Dumfries for at least 300 years, with the town boasting a green at the beginning of the eighteenth century. This photograph, taken c.1911, shows a match in progress on one of the public greens in Dock Park where, during the years leading up to the Second World War, you could play for the princely sum of 4d per hour (including the use of bowls and shoes).

THE PUTTING GREEN, DUMFRIES

There is a summer Sunday afternoon feeling to this 1920s' photograph showing townsfolk enjoying a leisurely game on the Dock Park putting course. A round of eighteen holes would have set you back 2d in those days.

When the White Star liner *Titanic* went down with heavy loss of life on 14 April 1912 during its ill-fated maiden voyage, many communities throughout the country were affected by the tragedy. Dumfries and Maxwelltown were no exception, as this memorial – fashioned out of Aberdeen granite and standing over 16 feet high – demonstrates. Erected in memory of band member John Law Hume and Thomas Mullin, a steward on the vessel, the obelisk was unveiled near the bandstand in Dock Park on 31 May 1913. 'Beautiful summer weather favoured the unveiling ceremony and

a great crowd of people assembled,' reported the local newspaper. 'During the forenoon the flags at the Midsteeple and Town Hall hung at half mast and before the hour of the ceremony the town bells were tolled. Amongst those present were relatives of the deceased lads.' A bronze panel bearing an engraving of the *Titanic* in relief can be seen above the inscription, with a scroll of music ('Nearer My God to Thee') cast in bronze set below on the moulded base.

Dumfries War Memorial is situated at the junction of Newall Terrace and Lovers' Walk. The memorial, which was unveiled on 9 July 1922 by Sir Francis Davies (Commander of Scottish Forces) was erected at a cost of £1,400 and is fashioned out of silver-grey Creetown granite. It stands 22 feet high, and the figure is of a King's Own Scottish Borderer in service dress standing with rifle reversed. 'The open air service at the unveiling was attended by a gathering of the townspeople

numbering close to six thousand,' reported the *Dumfries and Galloway Standard*. 'Crowds thronged Newall Terrace, Lovers' Walk and the Station Road, and in addition to those belonging to Dumfries and Maxwelltown, there were many who journeyed from the surrounding district.' The long roll of honour inscribed on the memorial's four panels includes the name of Dumfries woman Miss Roberta Ewart Robertson, who lost her life in an explosion at the Gretna munitions factory.

Benedictine Convent, Dumfries, Laboratory.

Pupils working in the well-equipped laboratory of the former girls' boarding school that was conducted by nuns at the Benedictine convent. The school was opened in 1887, three years after the convent had been established, and the first pupil to enrol eventually became Mother Superior in 1929. This photograph was clearly taken in the school's earliest days. The convent, which was described by the local newspaper as 'one of the most striking architectural objects in the landscape about Dumfries' stood in an elevated position overlooking the town and, as the large telescope seen here suggests, its grounds would have made an ideal spot for scanning the night sky. Astronomy perhaps formed a part of the broad curriculum which gave the school a reputation throughout Scotland for academic excellence. Although no longer a convent, the building (visible in the background of the picture on the left), still stands.

The War Memorial in Maxwelltown, standing at the junction of New Abbey Road and Rotchell Road in the shadow of the Benedictine convent on Corbelly Hill, was unveiled in November 1920. The bronze figure of a soldier with arms outstretched rests on a granite pedestal which records the names of over 200 men from the burgh of Maxwelltown and parish of Troqueer who died during the First World War.

Part of the sandstone quarry at Locharbriggs in the 1930s, showing a working platform and the heavy equipment used to hoist the sandstone from the quarry face. The quarry has been in existence – in one form or another – since about the early eighteenth century. Inevitably its fortunes have fluctuated over the years. Around 1900, for example, a local press report described how 'special trains and hundreds of bicycles conveyed the workers from Dumfries and the surrounding villages.' Hard times were to follow, however, when mechanisation and the falling demand for sandstone as a building material led to widespread unemployment, not only here but in the industry generally. In 1900, around 2,000 men were employed in Dumfriesshire's twenty or so sandstone quarries, but that number had plummeted to less than 300 by the outbreak of the Second World War. Throughout its long history the Locharbriggs quarry has been one of the main sources of building material in Scotland, and still produces sandstone that is widely noted for its rich red colour and durability.

Modern health and safety legislation has made roadside petrol pumps of the kind seen here at a filling station on the outskirts of Locharbriggs very much a thing of the past. It would be inconceivable – and indeed illegal – for petrol pumps to be sited in such close proximity to living accommodation in the present day and age. However, the cottage pictured here is still standing, although the pumps and general store have long gone. For motorists heading north out of the town on the A701, this would probably have been the last opportunity to fill up before reaching Porteous's roadside pumps at Beattock, twenty miles away.

The Arrol-Johnston motor works at Heathhall were once described as 'a little Detroit by the Nith.' The firm, established in 1898 with the manufacture of the Arrol-Johnston dog-cart, moved from Paisley to Dumfries in 1913 when large-scale expansion had been decided upon after the development of their 15.9 hp and 11.9 hp models. Dumfries was chosen as the location for the new works partly because of the town's proximity to important English markets, and also because it was conveniently placed near the main rail network for delivery of raw materials and despatch of goods. This side view of the works shows the large proportion of glass used in the construction of the building, giving the factory a truly striking (if not revolutionary) appearance for its time. Two hundred people were employed here at first, but within a year that number had more than doubled, with many skilled men being transferred from Paisley. Some houses (although many fewer than planned) were built nearby for the benefit of employees, but the bulk of the workforce had to find accommodation in the town.

Men leaving the Arrol-Johnston works at the end of a day-shift in 1913. Despite the dominating presence of the factory, Heathhall still managed to retain its rural aspect then. Following the First World War, during which over 1,000 men and women were employed at the works making aeroplane engines and munitions, production of motor vehicles was resumed and continued until 1929 when, after fluctuating fortunes and a merger with the Aster Engineering Company, car production ceased. It was a sad end to the high hopes that had been expressed on the works' opening day only sixteen years earlier. Then, relays of elegant Arrol-Johnston cars conveyed guests to and from the inaugural ceremony, with a special train also laid on for the purpose. In a fulsome speech, the Marquis of Graham declared that 'if there is such a thing as love at first sight, [these works] are certainly fitted to captivate us at first glance.' Several light engineering firms used parts of the works during the 1930s, and having been taken over by North British Rubber in 1946, they are now occupied by the Gates Rubber Company.

An engine belonging to the Caledonian Railway shown with its crew in the old goods yard and sidings outside Dumfries station. There was a time when the railway lines of south-west Scotland reached out from Dumfries to embrace some of the region's remotest areas. The first line to be opened (in 1848) was the Glasgow and South Western Company's Dumfries to Gretna Junction section of the route which eventually stretched westwards to Portpatrick, spawning branch lines to Kirkcudbright and Whithorn along the way. Fondly-remembered as the 'Paddy Line', this conveyed passengers to and from the Irish ferry, and linked up with the Caledonian Railway route to Glasgow at Gretna Junction. A line was also opened up from Dumfries to Glasgow and branch services were operated by the Cairn Valley Light Railway to Moniaive and also by the Caledonian Railway to Lockerbie. Now nothing remains except for the Dumfries to Glasgow route, which pushes on to connect with the main west-coast line at Carlisle.

The Craigs, photographed *c*.1908 when this area was very much a sylvan retreat outside Dumfries. It has since been encroached upon by the development and growth of Georgetown, but still affords extensive views across southern Annandale. Because of the area's lofty – and therefore healthy – position, a sanatorium was built on Craigs Road in 1905 in response to a smallpox scare in Dumfries. In the event it was destined never to receive a single smallpox patient, and the building (which was demolished in the early 1970s) later served as a TB hospital until the opening of the Lochmaben Sanatorium.

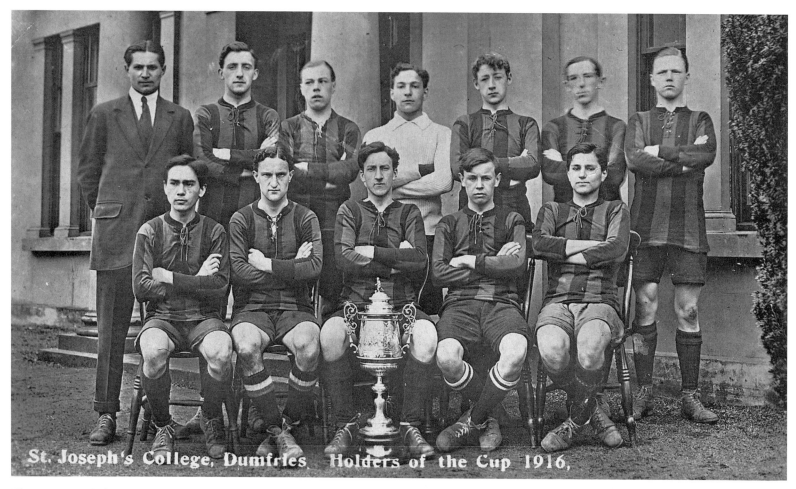

St. Joseph's College, Dumfries. Holders of the Cup 1916.

The winning side lines up with the cup, following a reunion football match at St Joseph's College between past and present pupils in April 1916, when the school's sixth form resoundingly beat the old boys 5–2. 'This event,' reported the local newspaper, 'which had been looked forward to with so much interest by the pupils, for a time hung in the balance on account of the weather, but towards midday the rain cleared away, and when the time came nothing but a strong wind blowing diagonally across the pitch, and a slippery surface, remained to affect the fortunes of the game.' In a poignant comment on the times, the newspaper went on to report that the match had a new referee for the first time in twelve years; the previous holder of that position having recently lost his life in the war.

Players, club officials, family and friends turned out for this photograph when Vulcan Rovers, a football team comprising employees of the Dumfries Motor Company, played a fixture against the Solway coast side Sandyhills at Huntingdon Park (now the site of St Mary's Industrial Estate). The two McKinnels played for Vulcan Rovers: Jimmy became manager of Queen of the South from 1945 to 1960, and John played junior football in Ayrshire.

A Dumfries Motor Company charabanc outing, 13 July 1930. The location of the photograph is unknown. Tom Johnstone (the 'busman'), who lodged for 62 years at 24 Queen Street, is pictured sitting in the front left seat.

Dumfries Town Band, 1909. The brass band, which is still thriving today with members of all ages, and performing at concerts, galas and the town's annual Guid Nychburris festivities, celebrated its centenary in 1995 (although the band may have existed under another name before 1885). The longest-serving member is Tommy Richmond, who played cornet with the band for 57 years (for sixteen years he was also the band's chairman) until his retirement in the early 1990s. At one time the band played on alternate Saturdays at the local football match, although it was claimed that every time they appeared Queen of the South lost! For many years the band had a practice hall in St Michael's Street, but they have now moved out to premises in Noblehill Park.

Vehicles lined up at Park Farm during the Royal Highland Show, July 1922. The show used to visit a number of different locations and came to Dumfries every eight years or so. The event pictured here marked the centenary of the first show (which was held in Edinburgh in 1822) and, as the local newspaper observed, 'a special pavilion was provided for lady members as a pleasant reminder of the occasion.' The press report went on to wax lyrical – and not without justification – about the setting of the venue itself. 'The admiration of the visitor is awakened by the majestic grandeur of frowning Criffel, and the location of the show has been the subject of much favourable comment amongst those visiting the Queen of the South for the first time.'

65 CASTLE DOUGLAS RD. MAXWELLTOWN.

Before the advent of the town's bypass, the Castle Douglas Road (seen here pre-1920), carried the burden of through traffic to Stranraer and all points west. The predominantly sandstone houses on the right-hand side of this residential road back on to the well-kept greens of Dumfries and Galloway Golf Club and Maxwelltown Bowling Green.

Looking south along Glasgow Street to its junction with Galloway Street *c.*1911. The old Glasgow Street School is pictured near right. Built in the mid-nineteenth century, the premises served as St Andrew's Roman Catholic Boys' School prior to their demolition around twenty years ago.

Glasgow Street looking north, *c*.1910. The small shops and houses seen here, so redolent of early-twentieth century Dumfries, have nearly all disappeared. After passing through the sprawling housing schemes of Lochside and Lincluden this road, from its busy junction with Galloway Street, forms the route out of town to Sanquhar and beyond.

3 NEW ABBEY RD. MAXWELLTOWN.

New Abbey Road in the early 1900s. These pleasing sandstone villas line the beginning of what is the A710 Solway Coast scenic route, which after meandering down through New Abbey and skirting the towering hump of Criffel pushes on to Dalbeattie. The old turnpike route through Galloway from Dumfries used to cut across this road at the bend (the low-roofed cottage just glimpsed on the left is now the 'Old Toll Bar Shop'). In a newspaper article dating from December 1965, Dr J. A. Russell explains that this route 'was an important one, as it connected finally with the packet-boat service from Portpatrick to Ireland. Once across the Nith into the Brig-en',' he continues, 'one reached the One-Mile Toll near Drungan's Lodge. Then it was on by Lochrutton and Milton of Urr.'

46

DICKSON'S DE-LUXE MOTOR TOURS

Two Dickson's de-luxe motor coaches awaiting departure from Whitesands. Jimmy Hood, leaning on the left-hand vehicle, started his own transport firm at Beeswing in the 1920s or 30s. Dickson's went out of business at the start of the Second World War when all their buses were requisitioned for use as ambulances. Both of these buses were built by Guy Motors of Wolverhampton.

G. H. Reed's multifaceted business comprising joiner, cabinetmaker, undertaker, antique dealer and house furnisher could be found at 114 English Street during the years before the Second World War. The hand-written message on the back of the older photograph (showing the doorway in the centre of the shopfront) reads: 'This is a photo of the old shop with Mr Reed at the door. It was taken prior to my appearance & as you will see by the window it was in very bad order.'